This Was Connecticut

Milford, 1902

T. S. Bronson

"This Was Connecticut"
Images of a Vanished World

Martin W. Sandler

In Association with The New Haven Colony Historical Society

L B

Little, Brown and Company   Boston   Toronto

All of the photographs in this book were printed
directly from the original glass plate negatives. In order to
preserve the integrity of the photographers' work, none of
the images has been retouched.

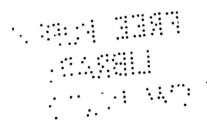

First Edition
T 04/77

Library of Congress Cataloging in Publication Data

Main entry under title:

This was Connecticut.

    Consists chiefly of photos. by T. S. Bronson and
others.
    1. Connecticut—Description and travel—Views.
2. Connecticut—Social life and customs—Pictorial works.
I. Sandler, Martin W.   II. Bronson, T. S.   III. New
Haven Colony Historical Society, New Haven.
F95.T47   974.6   76-75820
ISBN 0-316-77019-1

Published simultaneously in Canada by Little, Brown & Company (Canada) Limited
Printed in the United States of America

for Carol

Saybrook, c. 1890

Contents

Far Mill River, 1907   T. S. Bronson

Introduction

I have seized the light, I have arrested its flight.
With these words the Frenchman Louis Daguerre announced his success in capturing a photographic image on a copper plate. Daguerre's discovery, like those in so many other fields, was the result of a marvelous accident. He had been working on the problem for fourteen years. One day he took a plate that had been inadequately exposed in his crude camera and put it in a cupboard next to several bottles of acid. When he returned for the plate he found on it a vivid picture. The next day Daguerre put another plate in the cupboard. Twenty-four hours later he returned to find another clear photograph. What had happened was that mercury vapors in the darkened cupboard had acted on the underexposed copper plates in the same ratio to the amount of light to which the copper had previously been exposed.

In August of 1839 Daguerre proclaimed his discovery to the world. His announcement was not met with laughter or scorn. For, unlike many inventors, Daguerre had visible proof of his achievement. Excitement over the discovery was instantaneous and worldwide. In America Dr. Oliver Wendell Holmes called the camera "the mirror with a memory." The French artist Paul Delaroche exclaimed, "From today, painting is dead."

Daguerre was the first to offer proof of success in photography. He was not the first to achieve it. As early as 1827, another Frenchman, Nicéphore Niepce, had produced what he termed "the first picture from nature" with the use of a miniature camera he invented. (Niepce's photograph required an exposure time of eight hours.) And some months before Daguerre's success, an Englishman, William Henry Fox Talbot, had taken pictures of his house on paper sensitized by silver nitrate. Talbot's process was actually more far-reaching than Daguerre's.

The daguerreotype was a positive, a one-of-a-kind image. Talbot, on the other hand, had produced a negative from which countless copies could be made.

Within weeks after the announcements of the achievements of Daguerre and Talbot, people around the world began tinkering with photographic apparatus. The rise of photography was rapid. In 1851, Frederick Scott Archer devised a method by which glass plates could be coated with a thin film of collodion and potassium iodide and then dipped into a silver nitrate solution. Although these wet plates had to be developed within ten minutes, they produced images that have not been surpassed today. In the 1880's the dry plate process was perfected. This process was quickly followed by other major advances — including, of course, the invention that brought photography to the masses, George Eastman's Kodak camera with its flexible film.

The United States has produced a succession of true "masters of photography." We have come, more than ever, to appreciate their achievement and the high place they occupy in our cultural history. Southworth and Hawes (who were our leading daguerreotypists), Brady, O'Sullivan, Stieglitz, Steichen, Curtis, Berenice Abbott, Hine, Paul Strand . . . can anyone doubt that photography is an art form? Not if we have eyes to see.

With all respect to these acknowledged masters, however, I believe that there are nineteenth century photographers whose work has been unfairly neglected and who have earned the right to stand beside — or at least stand comparison with — the very best of their own time and of ours. Among New Englanders, Charles Currier is one such. The brothers George and Alvah Howe of Ashfield, Massachusetts, are two more. Porter Thayer and Baldwin Coolidge also belong on my list of unjustly forgotten masters of the photographic art.

The challenge, of course, is to find examples of an individual photographer's work in sufficient quantity to make an informed appraisal possible. Since the market for glass plate negatives was for decades virtually nonexistent and the interest of collectors correspondingly slight, only a small percentage of these fragile negatives has survived intact. Museums and historical societies have done the best they can to preserve negatives in their possession. But in terms of curatorial priorities, cataloguing and conservation of photographic materials have traditionally held low rank.

So the student of nineteenth century photography must be guided as much by faith and instinct, as by reason, in his archival researches. Like panning for gold, such research takes patience, a degree of physical stamina, and (if my own experience is any guide) lots of pure luck, if it is to produce significant results.

When I first visited the New Haven Colony Historical Society, I was seeking the work of no particular photographer. I was on a fishing expedition, pure and simple, hoping to find a striking negative or two that would help round out my forthcoming book *This Was New England*.

I was met at the Society by Rob Egleston and Assistant Curator Dave Corrigan, who were both relatively new to the Society and were involved in so many pressing projects that neither had yet had time systematically to go through the Society's negative collection (which was stored in an old kitchen in the Society's basement.) They bade me welcome, offered me the use of a light table, and left me in the middle of a sea of boxed negatives.

It was a familiar situation in which to find myself. I had already looked at a quarter of a million negatives for my New England book. New Haven was one of the last archives on my agenda. The strain was beginning to show; the joy of the chase was beginning to pall.

But I was less than halfway through the first carton of negatives when I turned to my wife, who, as in so many other searches, was working alongside me. Her eyes were as wide as my own. In this very first box, it was obvious, we had come across negatives of the highest quality and interest. And to make things even better, each negative was in an envelope on which the photographer had meticulously noted, in now faded, but still legible script, the date and subject of the photograph, the make of lens, exposure time, and type of plate used. Rob Egleston and Dave Corrigan quickly joined us, and we found ourselves almost recklessly exploring the hoard that lay around us. Here, truly, was a major collection of images of a vanished Connecticut by a master of his art.

A check of the acquisition records in the Society library revealed that the photographer was T. S. Bronson (1868 to 1955), a New Haven medical doctor who had been official photographer for Yale University and who also had been well known in his day as a musician. Subsequently we have learned that Dr. Bronson was a notable collector of cameras and photographic equipment — and the grandson of the founder of the New Haven Colony Historical Society.

It was fortunate that my New England book was practically finished, for my desire to introduce the work of T. S. Bronson to the public rapidly grew into an obsession. After a series of meetings with Joseph Johnson Smith, the dynamic young Executive Director of the Society, an agreement was reached and *This Was Connecticut* was under way.

I have now spent the better part of a year cataloguing the glass plate negatives in the Society's collection. It has been a tremendously exciting time for me. Finding negatives by photographers such as Myron T. Filley and George Bradley, who worked in earlier decades than did Bronson, has added much to the pleasures of my task. But the majority of the negatives, both at the New Haven Colony Historical Society and in this book, are by T. S. Bronson. He must have been an amazing man. How I wish I could have met him. Always the craftsman, always the seeker after perfection, he often shot exactly the same scene ten or even twenty times to capture the image he saw in his mind's eye. Bronson's love of the people of Connecticut was boundless. His love of the landscape no less so.

Selecting the photographs for *This Was Connecticut* proved a frustrating proposition. There are about 45,000 negatives of good quality in the Society's collection. Of these, I had prints made of 900. From these 900 prints, only 200 survived the final culling. I used four criteria for this final culling:

— the quality of the image in terms of composition and revelation of human character;

— the technical quality of the image (was the image scratched or stained, was the emulsion peeling, would it lend itself to duotone reproduction?);

— the documentary importance of the image;

— and, finally, the potential of a given photograph to convey that sense of time, place, and mood that seemed most representative of Connecticut in the years between 1855 and 1914.

In T. S. Bronson's time, as in our own, Connecticut was a photographer's delight. Already heavily industrialized, with a large urban population, it was still prime farm country. Its long coastline and inland waterways teemed with activity. The domestic and church architecture that distinguishes so many Connecticut towns today was everywhere evident in the nineteenth century — and was an obvious source of civic pride.

And Connecticut was, then as now, a prosperous state, the epitome of Yankee tenacity, inventiveness, and thrift.

Familiar as some of the scenes in this book may seem, however, to our own generation, the familiarity is often deceptive. The more one studies these photographs, the more one is seized by a not unpleasant sense of dislocation. We know these people, yet they are strangers to us. We have walked this land and sailed these waters, but with other maps and other charts.

The Connecticut of T. S. Bronson and Myron Filley and George Bradley has long since vanished. What remains is an image, captured on glass. The image alone reminds us that this *was* Connecticut.

Milford, 1902

T. S. Bronson

In Motion

This Was Connecticut is a visual document. It does not pretend to trace the formal history of nineteenth century Connecticut or even, in most cases, to give the history of the individual photographs being reproduced. Rather, it is an avowedly impressionistic portrait of Connecticut's people between the years 1855 and 1914 — where they lived, how they lived, the ways they worked, the ways they played, and what (to the extent a photographic image allows such speculation) they lived for. That the photographs reveal modes of life much different from our own goes almost without saying. Yet one must wonder that the onrush of time should separate us so completely from many scenes that would have been considered commonplace a scant half-century ago.

I have chosen to begin the book with photographs of Connecticut "in motion." For nowhere is the interplay between technology and social change more graphically demonstrated than in the transportation revolution that spanned the decades during which these photographs were taken. To be sure, old ways died hard, especially in rural sections of the state. The age of sail persisted through the age of steam. The age of the horse and buggy persisted into the age of the horseless carriage. But surely no one who was present that dramatic afternoon at New Haven's Lighthouse Beach (see pages 38–39) was blind to the meaning of manned flight. For the people of Connecticut, for all people everywhere, the dream had become reality.

There could be no looking back.

Oysterman, Hartford, 1901
Howes Bros.

Peddler, Hartford, 1900
Howes Bros.

New Haven, 1893

George Bradley

Robert Treat Memorial, Milford, 1906
T. S. Bronson

Milford, 1901
T. S. Bronson

Milford, 1906

T. S. Bronson

West Cheshire, 1909
T. S. Bronson

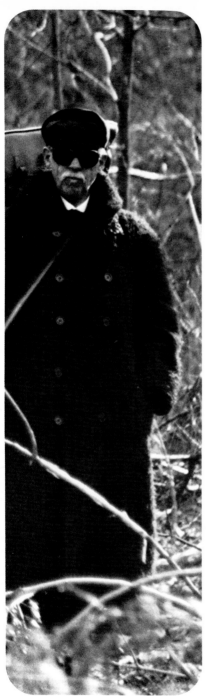

Details from photographs on pages 23 and 21

West Cheshire, 1909

T. S. Bronson

Milford, 1908

T. S. Bronson

Greenwich, 1909

T. S. Bronson

New Haven, 1909
T. S. Bronson

Smith on repair job, Fair Haven, 1909
T. S. Bronson

Westville, c. 1917

T. S. Bronson

Milldale, c. 1915
T. S. Bronson

Bridgeport, 1908

T. S. Bronson

Bridgeport, 1907

T. S. Bronson

Gravity railroad, New Haven, 1871
Photographer unknown

Westbrook 1906   T. S. Bronson

Engine #1, New Haven and Derby Railroad, 1871   Photographer unknown

Depot, Setago Lake, 1906

T. S. Bronson

Bridgeport, 1911

T. S. Bronson

Ferry, Lyme, 1908

T. S. Bronson

Lighthouse Point, New Haven, c. 1915
Photographer unknown

Gertrude L. Thebaud, *pride of the Gloucester fleet, envy of Long Island Sound*

Albert Cook Church

The Sea

It was no accident that the first European settlements in Connecticut were made along the Connecticut River. Easily navigable, running far inland through a richly fertile valley, the Connecticut River has remained for over three centuries a source of much of the state's wealth, power, and beauty. The long Connecticut coastline, sheltered as it is within Long Island Sound, has likewise provided the incentive for generations of ship-builders, sailors, and merchants to make their living from the sea. The number of coasting vessels, whalers, clippers, packets, fishing smacks, and steam and motor vessels that have hailed from Connecticut ports is past counting.

By the mid-nineteenth century, Connecticut's lakes, rivers, and coastal beaches were also becoming major recreational attractions. Sailing, swimming, or merely taking the salt air from the verandah of a summer cottage — the prospects of a day by the shore were obviously as enticing to early photographers as they were to the multitudes who endured the discomfort of woolen bathing costumes, horseflies, and sand-filled picnic lunches for the sake of a few hours of leisure.

These photographs underscore the extent to which the eye of the thoughtful photographer tends to govern what his camera records. That the ships and small craft depicted here should, for the most part, be shown in their handsomest light, that the dominant mood of the shore scenes should be one of good cheer and tranquility can hardly be accidental. Whether these images are objectively truthful is another question, which each of us will answer according to his own view of history and the human experience.

Double Beach, 1909

T. S. Bronson

Double Beach, 1909   T. S. Bronson

Double Beach, 1908
T. S. Bronson

Double Beach, 1908
T. S. Bronson

Lighthouse Point Beach, New Haven, c. 1915   T. S. Bronson

Lighthouse Point Beach, New Haven, 1906

T. S. Bronson

Lighthouse Point Beach, New Haven, 1906 T. S. Bronson

Westbrook, 1908

T. S. Bronson

Shipyard, Morris Cove, New Haven, 1907

T. S. Bronson

Regatta, Lamper's Cove, c. 1915   T. S. Bronson

Excursion boat at Bridgeport, 1903

T. S. Bronson

Launching of the Lucinda Sutton, *West Haven, 1891*   Photographer unknown

New Haven, 1902

T. S. Bronson

The Phantom, *c. 1910*
Photographer unknown

The Intrepid, *c. 1910*

The Traveler, on East Reef, Thimble Island, August 12, 1907   Photographer unknown

OVERLEAF: LEFT, *On the rocks, Stamford, 1884* [Myron T. Filley]; RIGHT, *Ashore, New London, c. 1910* [Photographer unknown]

Rose Garden, Elizabeth Park, Hartford, 1906

T. S. Bronson

Connecticut
Yankees

They were a proud, resourceful, inventive people, these Connecticut Yankees, with a decided predilection for tinkering with things mechanical and a seemingly inexhaustible capacity for building better mousetraps. They also gained a well-deserved reputation as shrewd traders (and diligent snake-oil salesmen). That Eli Whitney (albeit born in Massachusetts), J. P. Morgan, and P. T. Barnum had deep roots in Connecticut may have been coincidental. Less coincidental was Mark Twain's fascination with his Connecticut neighbors — or the fact that Hartford became the insurance capital of America and New Haven (with the help of another Eli) the seat of one of the world's greatest universities.

Making generalizations about the character of a people is a treacherous business at best. Although I have spent days and weeks studying the photographs from which this final selection was made, I cannot claim any special insight into the character of the individuals represented. I am, however, continually amazed at the range of emotions and moods these early photographs successfully capture. And I am no less impressed with the realization that the subjects of these photographs knew they were being recorded for posterity, that their expressions reflected this knowledge, and that early photographers shared in this knowledge and placed the greatest importance on it.

To see some part of ourselves in others is to make a beginning, at least, toward self-understanding. To see others as they would see themselves is to make a beginning, at least, toward mutual understanding.

Motorcycle, Mt. Carmel, 1908

Photographer unknown

New Haven, c. 1860
Photographer unknown

Bradley family, New Haven, c. 1885

George Bradley

Saybrook, c. 1895
George Bradley

Family group, Reading, c. 1890
Myron T. Filley

Seymour, 1893   Myron T. Filley

Detail from the photograph on the facing page

Spinning wool, Seymour, 1898
Photographer unknown

New Haven, c. 1870
Photographer unknown

New Haven, c. 1890
George Bradley

Westbrook, 1906

T. S. Bronson

Bicycle riders, Canaan, 1901
Howes Bros.

Aboard an excursion boat, Bridgeport, 1902
T. S. Bronson

New Haven, c. 1890   Myron T. Filley

New Haven, 1902
T. S. Bronson

Norwalk, c. 1895   George Bradley

Norwalk, c. 1895

George Bradley

Couple, Cornwall, 1906
T. S. Bronson

Stamford, 1904
T. S. Bronson

New Haven Camera Club, New Haven, 1906
T. S. Bronson

Mt. Carmel, 1909

T. S. Bronson

Couple, Middletown, 1907
T. S. Bronson

Primary school children, Woodmont, 1902
T. S. Bronson

Primary school children, Woodmont, 1902
T. S. Bronson

Hamden, 1907
T. S. Bronson

Hamden, 1907
T. S. Bronson

Milford, 1904

T. S. Bronson

Northfield, c. 1890   Myron T. Filley

Sharpening hoe, Saybrook, c. 1891   George Bradley

Enfield, 1902
Howes Bros.

Men's Club, New Haven, c. 1895   George Bradley

Private Japanese Garden, Mt. Carmel, c. 1895
George Bradley

William Howard Taft at Yale University, New Haven, 1908

T. S. Bronson

Lux et Veritas

Yale is not the oldest American university, or the largest, or the richest. One may nevertheless forgive those countless Yale alumni who have believed it to be the best. One such alumnus was T. S. Bronson, who, during his years as official Yale photographer, was indefatigable in seeking to capture the special spirit of "the college in New Haven."

Not for Bronson the stiffly posed class portraits so typical of the period. Bronson's eye was on the antic splendor of Yale's public celebrations, on the subtle interplay of character and setting that defined its more private world.

During Bronson's era, the athletic rivalry between Yale and Harvard was building dramatically — and was widely reported in the national press. If, in retrospect, this rivalry seems rather sophomoric, the pride it instilled among affluent alumni had a direct bearing upon the growth of Yale (and of course Harvard) as institutions of true intellectual distinction. For success on the playing fields had a way of easing purse strings. It made manifest a spirit of high achievement that even the most predatory Robber Baron could appreciate. The fleet of yachts that gathered every June for the boat races, the specially constructed "boat train" cars with their cheering spectators — these did not long survive the Great Depression. Yale survived, however, and we are all the richer for this legacy of cheering sons of Eli long since gathered to the grave.

The impact of Yale on the city of New Haven is more problematical. The division between town and gown has at times been very deep. The division still persists. But it is thanks in part to artists like T. S. Bronson that we can understand how much the citizens of New Haven gave to Yale.

Temple Street, New Haven, 1904
T. S. Bronson

Old Campus, Yale University, 1904   T. S. Bronson

Old Campus, Yale University, 1904
T. S. Bronson

Sheffield Scientific School, Yale University, New Haven, c. 1890

Yale University Medical School, New Haven, c. 1885

Myron T. Filley

Playing at marbles, Yale University, New Haven, 1901

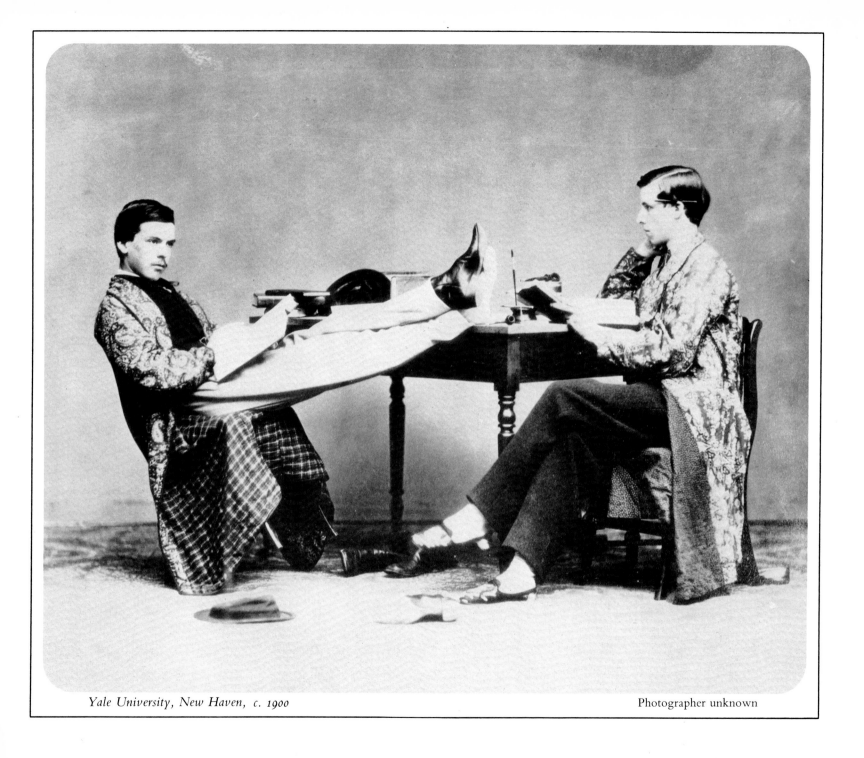

Yale University, New Haven, c. 1900

Photographer unknown

Yale Bicycle Club, Westville, c. 1870   Myron T. Filley

Yale Auto Hill Climb, Yale University, New Haven, 1908   T. S. Bronson

Yale University, New Haven, 1909

T. S. Bronson

Commencement Day, Yale University, New Haven, 1903

T. S. Bronson

Alumni reunion, Yale University, New Haven, 1908
T. S. Bronson

Tenth reunion class, Yale University, New Haven, 1908
T. S. Bronson

We love our
JINRIKISHAS
BUT OH
You Gin Rickeys

Alumni parade, Yale University, New Haven, 1908

T. S. Bronson

Yale boat train, New London, 1902
T. S. Bronson

Yale University, New Haven, 1912

T. S. Bronson

Class marshal, Yale University, New Haven, 1910

Yale-Harvard baseball, New Haven, 1908   T. S. Bronson

Yale-Brown football game, New Haven, 1911

T. S. Bronson

Half-time, Yale University, New Haven, 1911   T. S. Bronson

Yale-Princeton track meet, New Haven, 1911

T. S. Bronson

Yale launch, New Haven, c. 1890

Myron T. Filley

Yale-Harvard crew race, New London, 1906

T. S. Bronson

Yale crew, New London, 1868

Photographer unknown

Yale-Harvard crew race, 1908, New London
T. S. Bronson

Quarry workers, Granby, 1902

Howes Bros.

At Work

It was in New Haven, in 1798, that Eli Whitney conceived the first assembly line in America: a factory for the manufacture of firearms from largely standardized and interchangeable parts. Although mass production as we think of it today is obviously not unique to Connecticut, the range, variety, and ingenuity of nineteenth century Connecticut manufacturing enterprises — from Hitchcock chairs to hats, to inexpensive pocket watches, to heavy machinery — was a conspicuous feature of the state's economic life. The pool of skilled industrial labor in Connecticut, both native and foreign-born, built steadily through the nineteenth century, as the following photographs demonstrate. Meanwhile, draymen, tobacco farmers, oystermen, quarrymen, shipwrights, blacksmiths, carpenters, medical doctors, nurses, stockbrokers, tradesmen — and, not so coincidentally, photographers themselves — continued to attract the attention of the camera's eye.

The workers in these photographs were surely subject to the same frustrations and disappointments, and had the same strengths and defects of character, as their counterparts in other regions of the United States, then and now. But I do not believe it a misreading of the visual evidence to speak of a special sense of pride these men and women took in their work, in the performance of their craft. This pride is apparent in images in every section of *This Was Connecticut,* from the polished brass on the New Haven and Derby Railroad's Engine No. 1 or the immaculate paintwork of a delivery van to the quiet elegance of so much of Connecticut's domestic and public architecture.

Harsh masters and heavy discipline may get a job done fast. But self-mastery and self-discipline are higher virtues, often lifting even the lowliest laborers to achievements that partake of art.

Danbury, 1902

T. S. Bronson

Ready for picking, Suffield, 1903
Howes Bros.

Tobacco harvesting, Suffield, 1903
Howes Bros.

Haying, Farmington, 1902

T. S. Bronson

New Haven, 1908

T. S. Bronson

Waterbury, 1901
Howes Bros.

Hartford, 1901
Howes Bros.

THE SMEDLEY CO.
NEW HAVEN CONN.

MODERN FIREPROOF STOREHOUSE
FORWARDERS OF FURNITURE AND FINE GOODS.
TO ALL PARTS OF THE WORLD IN LIFT VANS.

THE SMEDLEY CO.
STORAGE
...ING
AND
...PING.

New Haven, 1902

T. S. Bronson

Chestnut vendor, New Haven, 1902
T. S. Bronson

Blacksmith's shop, Norwalk, 1902
Howes Bros.

Paving the street, New Haven, 1906

T. S. Bronson

Taken after the fire Jan 15 – 1867

After the fire, New Haven, 1867
Photographer unknown

Racing the engine, New Haven, 1872
Photographer unknown

Manning the engine, New Haven, 1882

Myron T. Filley

Grace Hospital fire, New Haven, 1908

T. S. Bronson

Ambulance, New Haven Hospital, New Haven, c. 1908   T. S. Bronson

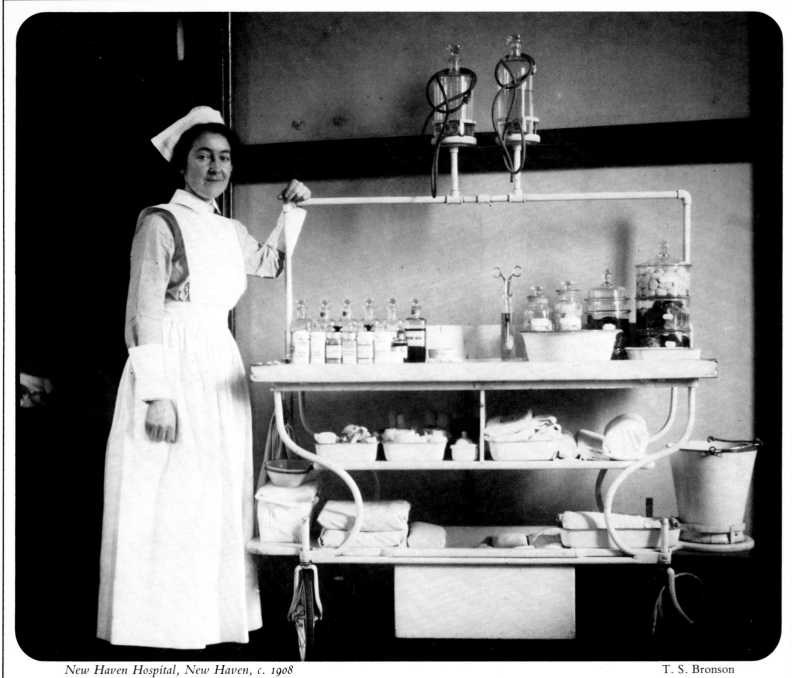

New Haven Hospital, New Haven, c. 1908   T. S. Bronson

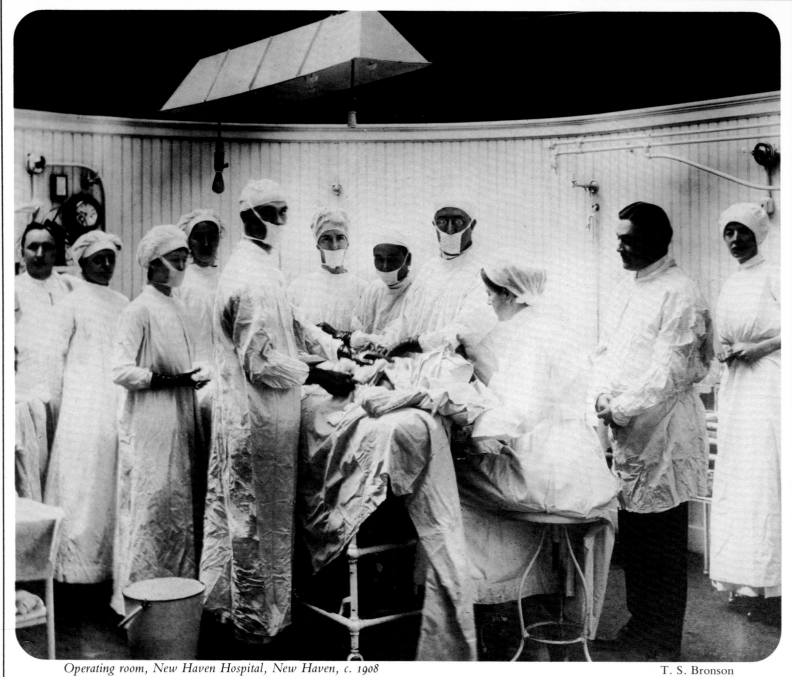

Operating room, New Haven Hospital, New Haven, c. 1908

T. S. Bronson

Physical therapy rooms, New Haven Hospital, New Haven, c. 1908   T. S. Bronson

Building a barn, Granby, 1902
Howes Bros.

Monument carvers, Hartford, 1901
Howes Bros.

Lumber yard, Somers, 1903

Howes Bros.

Lumber yard, Somers, 1903

Howes Bros.

Barn raising, Granby, 1902   Howes Bros.

Whitney Gun Factory, Hamden, 1902

T. S. Bronson

Building trolley tracks, Seymour, 1907
T. S. Bronson

Railroad yard, Fair Haven, 1903
T. S. Bronson

Telephone line crew, Fair Haven, 1902

T. S. Bronson

Snow removal, New Haven, 1906

T. S. Bronson

New Haven, 1908
T. S. Bronson

Auto show at Taft Hotel, New Haven, 1908
T. S. Bronson

Millinery shop, New Haven, 1906

T. S. Bronson

Stock brokers, New Haven, 1909   T. S. Bronson

Williams Orchestra, Lake Quanapaug, 1904

T. S. Bronson

Seymour, 1901

T. S. Bronson

Oyster boat, New Haven, 1903

T. S. Bronson

Mt. Carmel, 1908

T. S. Bronson

Newtown, 1904

T. S. Bronson

Fairfield, c. 1910

T. S. Bronson

At Play

Nostalgia makes for pleasing fantasy, but bad history. We may speak — indeed, I do speak — of the pride of workmanship, of the sense of order and place that characterized much of Connecticut life in the period covered by these photographs. Against all this, however, were the cruel realities of high infant mortality, of sixty-hour work weeks, of child labor, of subsistence wages (and nonexistent health and unemployment benefits), of poor sanitation, and of a succession of disastrous speculations, economic depressions, and bank failures that might humble even the richest and make destitute even the most thrifty and provident.

Under such conditions, it should follow that the people of nineteenth century Connecticut lived, as Thoreau would have it, "lives of quiet desperation." And perhaps they did — up to a point. Adversity, however, is a relative matter. Among the negatives at the New Haven Colony Historical Society, thousands of images testify to the fact that leisure was a big business in Connecticut from an early point and that a lot of people got a lot of enjoyment from their hard-earned dimes and dollars on their "day off." The photographs also remind us how ritualistic these nineteenth century Americans were in their pursuit of leisure and that club outings, formal picnics, skating parties, and Sunday promenades each called for particular forms of attire, and the observance of particular rules of etiquette.

From lakeside resort to city park, from backyard to Big Top — this was Connecticut at play.

Greenwich, 1906

T. S. Bronson

Harris Falls, 1908
T. S. Bronson

Far Mill River, 1907
T. S. Bronson

Lake Quanapaug, 1907

T. S. Bronson

West Hartford, c. 1915

T. S. Bronson

Bristol, c. 1915   T. S. Bronson

Woodstock, c. 1915   T. S. Bronson

Westbrook, 1907
T. S. Bronson

Bridgeport, 1907
T. S. Bronson

Double Beach, c. 1915   T. S. Bronson

Lake Quanapaug, 1911
T. S. Bronson

Picnic, Norwalk, 1910
T. S. Bronson

Double Beach, c. 1915
T. S. Bronson

County Fair, Berlin, 1904

T. S. Bronson

Circus grounds, New Haven, 1905

T. S. Bronson

Orange Fair, Orange, 1906

T. S. Bronson

Savin Rock Amusement Park, 1906   T. S. Bronson

Carnival, Branford, 1909
T. S. Bronson

Carnival, Branford, 1909
T. S. Bronson

Steam calliope, New Haven, 1907
T. S. Bronson

New Haven, 1903
T. S. Bronson

Derby Day, Derby, c. 1914   T. S. Bronson

Parade, Hartford, 1906

T. S. Bronson

Eagles parade, New Haven, 1902   T. S. Bronson

OVERLEAF: Detail from the photograph above

Lake Compounce, 1905

T. S. Bronson

Elizabeth Park, Hartford, c. 1915

T. S. Bronson

Westport, c. 1910

T. S. Bronson

Hammonassett Beach, c. 1915
T. S. Bronson

Lake Quanapaug, 1909
T. S. Bronson

Edgewood Park, 1904

T. S. Bronson

Lake Whitney, 1908
T. S. Bronson

Saybrook, c. 1890

A Sense of Place

Each community, each region, each nation
has a unique identity. What defines it in political or
economic terms may be — and often is — arbitrary and
subject to change. What defines it topographically is more
durable and palpable. But one thing is certain — those
who live or work within the boundaries of even the small-
est hamlet partake of "a sense of place." Without a sense of
place, our lives would be poor, indeed.

Connecticut is so varied a state that no one visual ele-
ment defines the whole. Nevertheless, the scenes that follow represent a conscious and deliberate attempt on the
part of the photographer to capture the particularities of
Connecticut life at a particular time in history. Even now,
it is possible, looking at such pictures, to share with the
photographer and his subjects a very real sense of place.
The photographs thus become far more than historical
documents. They remind us of the persistence of the past
in the present — they show us not only what we have lost,
but what such photographs help us to regain.

Let us hope that our own times are being captured
as faithfully and well.

Center Church, New Haven Green,
New Haven, 1908
T. S. Bronson

New Haven, c. 1890

George Bradley

Glastonbury, c. 1880

Myron T. Filley

Lebanon, 1909　　　　　　　　　　　　　　　　　　　　　Photographer unknown

North Madison, 1908

T. S. Bronson

Lyme, 1908

T. S. Bronson

Waterbury, c. 1900   Photographer unknown

Morris Cove, New Haven, 1906

T. S. Bronson

Manchester, c. 1880
Myron T. Filley

Seymour, 1895

Photographer unknown

Milford, 1907

T. S. Bronson

Filley House, New Haven, c. 1880

Myron T. Filley

Bronson House, New Haven, 1907

T. S. Bronson

New Haven, c. 1910

T. S. Bronson

New Haven, 1906

T. S. Bronson

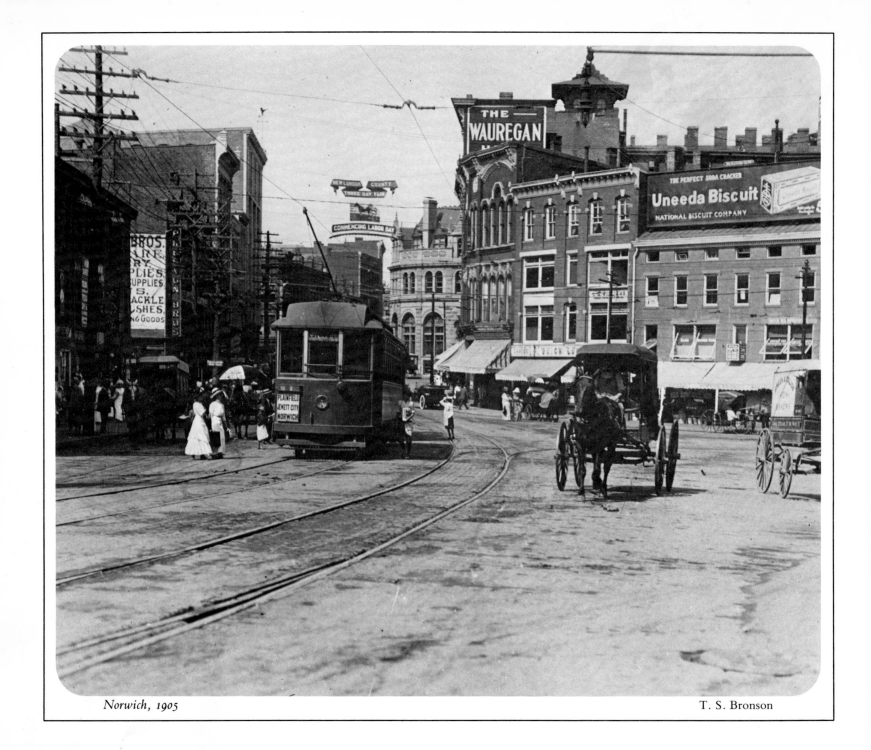

Norwich, 1905

T. S. Bronson

Savin Rock Amusement Park, 1908

T. S. Bronson

The Capitol, Hartford, c. 1905
T. S. Bronson

New Haven, 1907
T. S. Bronson

New Haven, 1902
T. S. Bronson

New London, 1907

T. S. Bronson

T. S. Bronson's mother, New Haven, 1907

T. S. Bronson

Bronson House, New Haven, 1906

T. S. Bronson

Orchestrian, New Haven, 1906

T. S. Bronson

Milford, c. 1905

T. S. Bronson

Sources

The great majority of photographs in this book are from the collection of the New Haven Colony Historical Society. But in order to give broader scope to this visual document of life in early Connecticut, other sources were used as well. These include the collection of Mrs. Edith LaFrancis (for the striking photographs taken by George and Alvah Howes), the Sterling Memorial Library, Yale University (for selected scenes of life at early Yale), and Mystic Seaport, Inc., Mystic, Connecticut. Photographs from these latter sources appear on the following pages:

Collection of Mrs. Edith LaFrancis: 16, 72 left, 88 left, 120, 121, 125, 128, 130 right, 140, 141, 142, 143.

Courtesy of Mystic Seaport, Inc., Mystic, Connecticut: 55, 56, 57, 59.

Sterling Memorial Library, Yale University: 100, 101, 102, 115, 117.

above: *T. S. Bronson Self-portrait, 1906*
below: *New Haven, c. 1905*
    T. S. Bronson

Designed by Mitchell Ford.
Calligraphy by Samuel Bryant.
Composed in Bembo and Blado
    by DEKR Corporation, of Woburn, Massachusetts.
Printed in two impressions
    by Eastern Press, New Haven,
    on Lustro Offset Enamel,
    a stock made by the S. D. Warren Company
    and supplied by Carter, Rice, Storrs, and Bement.
Bound in Columbia Mills' Fictionette book cloth
    by A. Horowitz and Son, Fairfield, New Jersey.